SEIZING
MOMENTS of
Possibility

Ways to *Trigger Energy* and *Forward Momentum* on Your Ideas and Plans

RICK MAURER

PARZIVAL PUBLISHING • ARLINGTON, VIRGINIA

For information, contact:
Parzival Publishing
P.O. Box 50142
Arlington, VA 22205

Paperback ISBN: 978-1-7369567-0-0
ebook (PDF) ISBN: 978-1-7369567-1-7
Library of Congress Control Number: 2021907878

Design and layout by: Jamie Tipton, Open Heart Designs

"'Tain't What You Do
(It's the Way That You Do It)"

–Song by **SY OLIVER** and **TRUMMY YOUNG**

Contents

This is a quick, five-question self-assessment that will allow you to determine if my book is a good fit for you. Why waste your time on something you don't need?

Energy can propel a big change forward successfully, or energy can work against you and destroy the best-laid plans. In this chapter, I identify the types of things that can drain excitement and commitment. And I show you what it takes to steer clear of those common mistakes.

Observing is key. In this chapter, I show you how to recognize energy in action, in real time. You will improve your ability to spot what's working, and what's working against you. Your ability to pick up these signals—and they are everywhere—will be key to building and sustaining strong support for new ideas, projects, and other organizational changes.

Photographers often carry kitbags filled with lenses. Each lens allows them to see a scene from a different perspective. We need kitbags like that when we attempt to understand and influence others. I go over a few of the lenses that I use and that my clients have found useful.

Finding easy ways to blend in energy—getting people talking and engaged, helping you explore the pros and cons—is a great way to add juice and vitality to your ideas and plans. And starting simply can help keep you and the people you want to influence in your respective comfort zones—and that is a big deal.

I have identified how a few powerful centers or pockets of energy can work for you or against you during a big change. I will show you how to avoid things that undermine your efforts and instead create strategies that trigger positive energy and strong forward momentum.

Even though this book focuses on big projects at work, the things I've learned (and continue to learn) about what it takes to treat others with dignity and respect and staying open to them and their points of view has helped me far beyond the workplace. I hope you will find these thoughts useful as well.

Why I Wrote This Book

I asked a leader in a large organization to imagine that we were in a bar at the end of the day so that we could just talk informally. I asked her, "How are things going on that big project?"

She shook her head and said, "Why don't people @#$ing get it?"

When I told other leaders that story, they often nodded and added their own choice profane comments. They told me about big changes that never got off the ground and times when they couldn't get some small group of people upstairs interested in their ideas.

I was confused. There is no shortage of fine resources out there on ways to influence others, to lead and manage organizational changes and projects. And I knew that many of these leaders had read the same books and heard the same speakers as I had.

When I asked those men and women what went wrong, they could tell me, without hesitation. And if I asked, "What could you or those other leaders have done differently?" they had good answers for that question as well.

If those leaders knew what they needed to do and know how to do it, why weren't more big projects successful?

Then I had a wakeup call. I realized that one big thing was missing from all those good plans and resources. Not one of them ran on its own. All those great resources should include little stickers on the back that read WARNING: BATTERIES NOT INCLUDED.

Think about this: Maybe the plans you are using today are fine, but they might need serious infusions of energy to get things moving and stay fully charged from the beginning to the end.

The key is to seamlessly blend energy and forward momentum into everything you do related to a new idea. If your plans and strategies call for big planning meetings, conference calls with a few others, routine "fill out the forms" meetings, or simply informal discussions about some aspects of the project, you will need to make sure that they are all conducted in ways that can harness energy productively.

Every one of those events is an opportunity to increase energy and strong forward momentum.

I wrote this book to help you *Seize Moments of Possibility.* I will show you how to recognize opportunities to harness energy that you might have missed in the past and how to seamlessly blend those moments into your existing plans.

Rick Maurer

Should You Read This Book?

I wrote this book for individuals who are responsible for leading (or advising men and women who are leading) projects and changes inside organizations.

I believe that building support begins with you and me. We need to understand what support for change feels like when it is present and helping drive things forward—and what is feels like when energy is low or working against us.

Here are a few questions that can help you decide if you ought to spend some time reading and exploring the ideas I present in *Seizing Moments of Possibility.*

QUESTION 1: How important is it for you to be able to build and sustain strong support for your ideas, changes in the organization, and/or projects? (By support I mean a high commitment and the energy to create strong forward momentum.)

1_____2_____3_____4_____5
LOW   HIGH

QUESTION 2: How willing are you to be influenced by the people whom you want to influence?

1_____2_____3_____4_____5
LOW   HIGH

QUESTION 3: How would you rate the importance your organization gives to building and sustaining strong support? You might think about your entire organization, a division, a professional specialty such at IT or HR, or the team you work with directly. If you are a consultant or coach, then consider focusing on one client organization.

1_____2_____3_____4_____5
LOW   HIGH

QUESTION 4: To what extent do you believe that building support begins with you?

1_____2_____3_____4_____5
LOW   HIGH

QUESTION 5: How would you rate your effectiveness in building and sustaining strong support for new ideas, big projects, and organizational changes?

1_____2_____3_____4_____5
LOW   HIGH

Understanding your scores:

If you scored high on Question 5, you might enjoy the book, and you might pick up a few tips, but I didn't write it for you. You are already skilled at the human part of change. And congratulations—not a lot of people are skilled in this area.

If you scored 3 to 5 on Questions 1 through 3, then I think you'll find some useful ideas and tools in this book.

Do you believe that building support begins with you? (Question 4) If you scored high, you might find a lot of ideas that can help. If you scored 1 to 3, the ideas in my book might bring you around to reassess your role. But frankly, if you read and try out the ideas in Chapters 1 through 3, and you still don't believe that support begins with you, then you can put the book down. This approach is probably not for you.

CHAPTER ONE

Why Is Lack of Energy So Deadly, and How Can You Avoid the Problems It Creates?

"I've learned from my mistakes.
I'm sure that I could repeat them exactly."

–PETER COOK, from the "Frog and Peach" routine

If I were to ask you why it's so hard to build the support you need for projects and other changes, you might answer:

✔ Projects eat up way too much of my time. There are too many moving pieces, conferences, setbacks, and meetings that don't add much (if any) value.

✔ I try to get people involved, but when push comes to shove, it is so much faster to do it myself or pull a small group together to get the job done.

✔ Sometimes I assume that all it takes is a good idea, and everything else will fall into place. I believe that once people understand what's going on, they will go along. In fact, they might even thank me for getting things started without "wasting" their time.

✔ Getting people involved seems soft. I know it's important, but I think it will make me look soft—and there is no place for that where I work.

✔ I believe that because the project or change-management plan we are about to use is so comprehensive, all any of us will have to do is follow it step by step, and we will reach our goals successfully, on time, and within budget.

Any one of those beliefs can get in the way of building a strong base of support for your new ideas, projects, or other big changes. The good news is that we can often avoid those setbacks if we simply pay attention to the impact these activities can have on building the support we will need.

Let's just take the first item on that list: Projects eat up way too much of my time. That's probably true. But ask yourself how many of those meetings and calls and reports and so forth fail to move projects forward in any meaningful way. Then ask, what if people were more engaged, more willing to volunteer to help move things ahead, or even wanted to become champions for making these projects a success? I believe our job is to look for opportunities to seize moments of possibility.

What Can Build a Foundation for Strong Support?

You. I truly believe that it all begins with you.

Understanding what gets people interested and willing to work with you can be critical to seeing moments of possibility and using them to your advantage. What you do in those moments will determine the ebb and flow of energy throughout your work together.

A QUICK WAY TO IDENTIFY WHAT GETS PEOPLE EXCITED AND ENGAGED

Here is a simple activity I have used with clients over the years to jumpstart that understanding. I encourage you to slow down for a few minutes and try it out.

Think about a job that you had (it could be your current job) that made you happy. You loved going to work. That doesn't mean you loved every minute of the work, but you loved most of those minutes and hours and days and years.

Please grab a piece of paper and jot down what was it about that job that made you so happy.

Here is my own response to those questions.

▶ **WHAT WAS THE JOB?**

I played in a jazz quartet in college. Almost every Saturday we had a gig in the Chicago suburbs. These were often wedding receptions, but as long as people could dance, they didn't seem to mind that we improvised along the way.

▶ **WHAT DID YOU LIKE ABOUT THE JOB?**

A lot! I liked the guys I played with. They were great guys and fine musicians. We respected each other and enjoyed each other's company.

One treat was that we often went to an all-night diner and hung with other musicians and talked about music, Chicago sports, and all the other things young men talked about.

We challenged ourselves by adding new tunes and working to make them sound as good as we could for our audiences. (We could tell if we were succeeding by how many people stayed out on the dance floor when we played.)

▶ **WHAT CONNECTIONS DO YOU SEE BETWEEN THAT IDEAL JOB AND THE BIG PROJECT YOU ARE ABOUT TO BEGIN? IN THE LIST YOU JUST CREATED, THERE ARE LIKELY KEYS TO WHAT CAN HELP YOU BUILD SUPPORT FOR CHANGE AND OTHER PROJECTS.**

In my example, it didn't make any difference who got the gig and was therefore the leader for that evening; we acted like a self-organizing team. It was hard to tell who the leader was, since we all listened to each other and built on each other's ideas and playing. We had a pretty good way of telling if we were successful: people danced or turned and actually listened, and often they asked if we'd be interested in playing for some event that was coming up. If our music wasn't working on any given night, it would feel like we were playing for the heads carved in Mount Rushmore.

▸ You will find worksheets for all of the Application Activities as well as other resources at www.rickmaurer.com/MofPResources

You certainly could have chosen the job you have today for this exercise, but I've had people tell me their most satisfying job was as a lifeguard, a fighter pilot, a nuclear engineer, and on and on. In fact, I once asked a client who had been a roadie for The Grateful Dead what made him happy at work. It was a great answer, but I can't print it here.

A key to finding and taking advantage of moments of possibility rests in our ability to draw on our own experiences. You'll probably be going into a face-to-face or virtual meeting sometime today.

While you are attending the meeting, just ask yourself, *Does this meeting or this work fit my own criteria for what I find satisfying?* That kind of quick reflection can serve you well as you begin to apply the ideas in this book.

This is Application Activity #1 in this book. You will find one or more of these activities in each chapter. I hope you will slow down for a few moments and complete each one. I added these activities to help you understand the material more deeply so you can begin to see how these ideas relate to your *Seizing Moments of Possibility.*

Think of it this way. If I were coaching you, I would be suggesting ways to try out what we've been talking about. So think of these activities as coaching sessions that don't cost you anything.

It All Begins with You

Moments of possibility are present almost all the time. For instance, the last item on the list of obstacles to gaining support is just assuming that a great, comprehensive plan is all you need. Not so. Every step in that plan has the potential to work in a way that not only completes the task but also builds support in the process. It is just too easy to assume that simply going through the steps is all you need to do to build support. Maybe you've watched a cooking show and thought, *I can do that!* So you bake that magnificent cake, but it doesn't look like the one you saw the master chef put together. As for support: people were polite, but no one asked for seconds or wanted a copy of the recipe.

Two years ago, I conducted a study titled *Are All-Hands Meetings Worth the Bother?* Thirty percent of the respondents said that those meetings were a good use of time. But seventy percent said they could have been much more effective. Complaints were that these large meetings were unfocused, and agendas covered nothing new. Top-down and one-way communication dominated the meetings—too much telling and not enough listening. Some said such meetings generated more questions than they answered.

You have probably attended many large meetings that have wasted people's time. The good news is that they have given you a wealth of valuable experiences. I imagine you can easily identify five or six things that could have made those big meetings come alive. Those memories can help you begin to build a repertoire of moments-of-possibility material to draw on.

Imagine you are in a group that is planning a big town-hall event as part of an important project.

As you walk into the planning meeting, you remember those big events that people said were a joke. Almost immediately, you can picture things that with just a little tweaking could have improved those gatherings. The leaders could have...

- Identified a clear and compelling goal for the meeting.

- Limited presentations to a fraction of the allotted time.

- Decided what they wanted to learn from people coming to the meeting.

- Come up with a simple way to ask for participation from the full group in a way that was safe for everyone.

Any of your memories of bad meetings gone by can be a catalyst for doing it right this time as you design your own event.

Seizing moments of possibility is nothing fancy. It's the same room. The same people. The same bad coffee. All you've done is come up with ways to use that time together more effectively. You took advantage of moments of possibility just waiting to be seized.

And now, a personal bad example. . .

One of my first consulting assignments was to plan and facilitate an off-site meeting between management and labor in a government agency. I was excited. All that learning I had done was going to pay off.

We all arrived at the three-day, off-site meeting. I asked people to introduce themselves. So far, so good. And then things got bad.

Real bad. People started pointing fingers and accusing each other of rotten things. *But,* I thought, *I am a trained facilitator. Like Midas, I can turn all this nastiness into gold. Just watch me.*

But before that magic could happen, they all turned on me. They hurled insults. They yelled. I felt like I was in the ring with Mike Tyson in his prime.

Imagine that I had slowed down just a bit and thought, *Hmmm, a three-day, off-site between two groups that don't like each other. Gee, I wonder if anything could go wrong?*

A moment of reflection like that while I was planning the event could have changed everything. I could have called the respective leaders beforehand and asked for more input about what prompted this meeting and what they wanted to accomplish. I could have asked for their help in planning and maybe facilitating the meeting. And was an off-site event even the best use of their time and energy? (In Chapter 2, I'll tell you how—with some adult supervision—I got out of that mess and actually provided a little value to those two teams.)

In Chapters 2 and 3 I will suggest ways to begin to spot moments of possibility to get energy and momentum going. And then in Chapters 4 and 5 I will suggest ways that you can turn those observations into actions that can begin to build support and forward momentum into your plans from beginning to end.

But one last thing in this chapter, and it has to do with coffee.

Think Like a Good Barista

What if you could get support growing right from the beginning? What if you recognized that every meeting, every conference call, and every step along the way was an opportunity to create or sustain the support you will need?

In *Seizing Moments of Possibility*, I will show you how to blend support and forward momentum into your plans and daily activities. And, in the process, not only can you build strong support, but you will probably save a lot of time.

In case you are skimming this book, you may want to read that last sentence again. Blending support into your activities might actually save you time—and headaches!

Here's what all that has to do with coffee.

When I go to my local coffee shop, invariably there is someone in line who orders a latte. I've never once heard that person say, "Give me a latte, but hold the milk." You can't do that. Espresso and steamed milk are the two essential ingredients. Without both of them, you don't have a latte.

And when a latte is made by a skilled barista, you can't tell where the milk ends and the coffee begins. Those lattes are a seamless blend of goodness.

I am *not* going to suggest that you start using a new plan or even add additional events to your busy schedule. But I am going to strongly suggest that you find ways to infuse energy into things that you are already doing. I'd like to show you how to find ways to act like a barista and blend human aspirations and needs into the technical part of your plans.

You might also see places where your plan is missing opportunities to build support, and so you might decide to add in additional activities. That can make sense, but please don't start with the extras. Growing support for your ideas and plans really does begin with you, right here and right now.

I think you will find that even the most pedestrian and routine meetings have many moments of possibility that don't have to add time or hassle to your life.

Getting the Most from This Book

LeBron James did not become a basketball superstar by spending his days watching instructional videos on YouTube. I don't think Yo-Yo Ma became a master cellist by spending lots of hours watching videos either.

Passive learning can be tempting. In fact, I just checked Google and learned that you can watch videos that promise to teach you macramé, decoupage, golf, bagpipes, taxidermy, snooker, chess, and the list goes on. Those videos, similar to a book like this, can be helpful in giving you some information and pointing the way. But if you want to improve your skills in macramé or bagpipes, you'll need to practice too.

Observation, practice, and reflection on how you are doing are key to learning a skill. As you've already seen, I inserted some quick Application Activities throughout this book to help you take advantage of the ideas and tools I discuss. I encourage you to take the time to address those activities. I don't think you will regret it.

As you move on to Chapter 2, please use that list that you just created in Application Activity #1 and think about the project or big change that prompted you to read this book. As you think about the project, which of those items that made you happy are likely to be present? And which ones might be missing if you are not careful?

Then put yourself in the shoes of others who will have a stake in this work and ask the same question: Which of the items from that list are likely to be present for them? I encourage you to think about a wide sample of potential stakeholders as you reflect on this.

Key Points in Application Activity #1:
Quick Ways to Get People Excited and Engaged

→ What was the job?

→ What did you like about the job?

→ What connections do you see between that ideal job and the big project you are working on?

→ While you are attending meetings, working on reports, etc., ask yourself if these activities meet your criteria of satisfying.

CHAPTER 2

Spotting Moments of Possibility

"You can observe a lot just by watching."

–YOGI BERRA, baseball legend and worldly philosopher

Yogi was right. You can observe and learn a lot just by watching. And too often we can be so action-oriented that we overlook this vital resource.

Taiichi Ohno is often referred to as the founder of the Toyota Production System. One important aspect of his approach is the Ohno Circle. He would draw a circle on the floor, and your job was to stand and observe what was going on around you for hours. Yes, you read that right—for hours!

He would sometimes come by and ask questions like: Why are they doing that? What is that tool used for? What are they doing now? And so on. And if you didn't know the correct answers, you might have to stand there for another few hours.

I had the opportunity to experience a mini-version of an Ohno Circle at a production facility. I was told to stand quietly and observe a workstation for about thirty minutes. It was fascinating. I noticed a rhythm in the movement of employees. I saw one person do something at a workstation and then take five or six steps to pick up a new piece to work on. That person repeated that exact process a few times while I watched. But the big lesson came when the instructors asked us to debrief. It was then I realized how much I had missed.

It seemed to me that much of what was working—and not working—was hidden in plain sight.

Even learning to observe a little bit better can have a profound effect on the options available to us.

This book is not filled with a lot of theory or step-by-step recipes for building stronger support. The book is much simpler than that. I am suggesting that much of what we need to see and do to build support and forward momentum is right in front of us if we simply pay attention.

The Challenge of Observing

Psychologist Daniel J. Simons and colleagues created a fascinating experiment. They assembled a group of people to watch two groups pass a basketball. Not shoot, not dribble, but simply pass. The task for the observers was to count how often one particular team passed the ball.

At the end of this brief activity, they asked the observers how many times the people in white jerseys had passed the ball. Some got the number correct; many others were close. So far, so good. Then the researcher would ask how many noticed the gorilla. Often, over half the observers failed to notice a person in a gorilla suit walk onto the court and stand there.

Since I knew about that experiment, I was ready. I knew to count the passes but also to look for the gorilla. Those researchers weren't gonna fool me. But then one of them asked, "How many of you noticed a player wearing a black jersey walk off the stage when the gorilla entered?" I missed that.

He then asked how many of us saw the curtain behind the players change color during the activity. I didn't see that one either.

We are often good at paying attention to what we believe is important. That's a good thing, but that same intense focus on the task at hand—counting how many times a team passes a ball—can get in the way of our ability to see gorillas walking in and people leaving the meeting. (To learn more about these experiments, go to the Resources section of this book.)

What gets in the way? Imagine that we are called into a meeting to discuss a mounting cash flow crisis in our organization. We probably understand the importance of that meeting and do our best to try to help the group come up with some way to reverse the problem. After all, isn't that the reason for the meeting?

But suppose you and I were in that meeting and failed to notice that representatives from the finance department were completely silent. Could people who work with finances every day have something to add to this conversation? We'll probably never know, because we didn't notice that they were saying nothing, and that's because our attention was on columns of numbers.

My friend John Mariotti was head of Huffy Bicycles back when a quality movement was taking off in the US. Huffy made bikes for kids and families. Basic bikes. But they had a lot of competition. Leaders at Huffy decided to start a quality-improvement process while lowering costs. (Often higher quality and lower cost were treated as opposite ends of a polarity in organizations.)

I asked John why it worked so well. He said, "We impressed on employees that quality could not be compromised. As we improved quality, we saved money. We saved in warranty costs and product liability, and we reduced waste in the operation."

Here's where observing comes in. I asked him what happened to supervisors and managers when employees were given so much more power. He said they had left those men and women out of the loop at first. Many of the frontline leaders were very good working in an old autocratic environment. "Unfortunately, we categorically classified them as the wrong kind of person for this new way of doing things," Mariotti said.

The senior leaders just assumed that since these supervisors were older, they were set in their ways. And then one of the executives said, "Did anyone ever explain to the first-line supervisors why we need to improve quality and why they are critical to our success?" The answer was no.

They talked with the first-line leaders. Most of those supervisors weren't aware of how critical it was for Huffy to find a way to distinguish their bikes from all that competition. Many of the supervisors got it. They got on board and became strong advocates for making quality improvement a success.

I don't think it is a coincidence that Huffy's financial performance grew stronger, while Schwinn, their biggest competitor, sank into bankruptcy.

Failure to notice their natural leaders—the people who probably had the best relationship with hourly employees—was a missed moment of possibility.

Maybe our brains are too full to see new things.

If we are paying close attention to the task at hand—like cash flow issues or counting passed balls—we are likely to tune out other stimuli. Or, if we enter meetings with the mindset that only executives make executive decisions, we may have difficulty observing possibilities just waiting to be tapped.

Dr. Debbie Crews, a researcher in sports psychology, conducted an interesting experiment with golfers. She assembled two groups. One group included golfers who were consistently good at putting. The other group was people who did not sink their putts consistently.

She had the players wear special headsets that recorded brain activity. When golfers from both groups walked up to the hole, there was a tremendous amount of brain activity on both sides of their brains. But when the better golfers got ready to putt, their brain activity changed dramatically.

The inconsistent putters still had a lot of brain activity going on. Perhaps they were thinking about the slight breeze and what impact that might have on the shot. Maybe they were noticing that the grass was still a little wet and wondering how that might affect the path of the ball. They might have been thinking about how they were standing and holding their club. Or maybe they were simply hoping to make the putt.

It doesn't make much difference what they were thinking; the point is that their brains were busy. The better putters had far less brain activity in that final second. They were calmer. As Dr. Crews said, ". . . it was the last second of data that was predictive of performance." (For more about her work, please visit the Resources section of this book.)

Dr. Crews went on to say that when the better golfers finished their decision-making, they would "walk up (still doing important processing), setting the club, looking to see if the alignment was correct, et cetera," but then the left side of the brain quieted as they hit the ball.

How does this apply to us at work? It's not at all uncommon for people to go from meeting to meeting with virtually no break in between. So as the ten o'clock meeting is starting, we're still thinking about things from the last meeting. And perhaps we get a text during this meeting that distracts us a little bit. Maybe we are looking at the packed agenda for the ten o'clock meeting and wondering how we'll ever get through it all. And as the meeting is ending, we have already begun to switch our attention to the next meeting, which will start in ten minutes.

We may find ourselves in meetings where we wonder if it is safe to say something without taking a political risk or hurting the boss's feelings. We can see potential moments of possibility, but we dare not speak. Chris Argyris conducted important research on executive teams. He found that there were often lots of "undiscussables" in meetings, and these verboten topics had a negative impact on performance. (For more about Argyris's work, visit the Resources section.)

I mentioned this concept to a senior team that was struggling. They let out one of those laughs of recognition, and then, much to my surprise, they started talking openly about those things that had been undiscussable only a few minutes earlier. Their awareness of the power of undiscussables opened the door to more productive ways of communicating with each other on some key issues.

Increasing Our Ability to Observe

Mark Helias, the great jazz bassist, was once asked what he thought about when he was on a gig. Mark tends to play in very adventurous groups where a lot of what the audience hears is being created on the spot. Yes, it's jazz, but it's jazz at the highest level, where the players in the combo must listen deeply to each other to collectively create what's going on moment to moment. They aren't thinking about the structure of the song, the harmonic movement, how they should finger a particular passage, or any of the many other things that go into getting ready to play.

What does Mark Helias think about when he's on the stage with other musicians? In a workshop at the Creative Music Studios in Woodstock, New York, he said, "I don't think about anything. I can't even remember my name. . . but when I'm practicing, I'm thinking all the time."

Similarly, I know a New York jazz musician who said that if you walked into a jam session at a major club carrying a book that included written music for a lot of jazz standards, you would be branded as an amateur and probably would not be invited to play. There might be some arrogance at play, but more important, it is difficult for most musicians to focus on listening and responding to each other with anything close to full attention while trying to read sheet music at the same time.

I hope you are seeing that our brains can work overtime and get in the way of *Seizing Moments of Possibility*. In Chapters 4 and 5, I will cover ways to turn those observations into productive actions, but for now I'd like to stick with ways to open ourselves to observing a fuller picture.

Clearing Your Mind

Just like the golfers in Dr. Crews's studies, we need ways to allow ourselves to be fully present when we're engaging others on topics that are important to us. But first, we need to be calm enough to see those gorillas right in front of us.

Sometimes, it can be as simple as taking a breath.

Of course we're going to breathe, but how often do we actually pay attention to the breaths we take? Imagine you are about to log in to a meeting that is likely to be contentious. What if you simply took a breath or two and allowed yourself to take Yogi Berra's advice—just watch.

As the meeting goes on, you allow yourself to pay attention to your breath. You might feel calmer and start to see things you had missed in how people are talking to each other—or not. You might realize that there are no good places where you can bring up something important to you today. That's important information. Or you might begin to see potential moments where you could say something.

When I've been around good martial artists, they always seem calmer and more in control than me. At least that's the way it always appeared as I looked up at them from the floor.

Like good golfers, master martial artists enter situations more calmly than the rest of us. We can learn from them.

Clearing Our Minds by Focusing Intently

One study examined basketball players as they went for three-point shots. One thing distinguishing players who made these throws successfully from those who didn't was the amount of time they took actually looking at the basket before they made the throw. They call this "quiet eye." This intense focus is measured in milliseconds.

At the beginning of this chapter, I said that observing can be deceptively difficult. It can also be deceptively easy if we simply pay attention to how we pay attention. The point is that these masters can clear their minds by keeping their focus on where they want the ball to go.

Looking with Soft Eyes

I don't recall where I first got the advice to look with soft eyes, but I love it. It suggests to me that I should focus on what's going on and also stay open to other things that might grab my attention. A gorilla walking on stage, for instance.

There is a concept in psychology called figure/ground. It refers to the tendency of the visual system to simplify a scene into the main object that we are looking at (the figure), and everything else forms the background (or ground).

You may have ridden in cars with people who get very nervous, and their attention seems to be limited to what is directly in front of them, so they miss information that could be coming at them from off to the sides.

I don't like driving in snow, and there have been many times when I've had to drive the Pennsylvania Turnpike very late at night during big storms. I could feel my body tense. My hands clutched the wheel. As you probably know, that's a pretty dangerous thing to do. At any moment, your car could start to skid, and you need to allow it to skid a little to keep it moving forward.

Over the years, I learned to remind myself to use soft eyes, or in this case, soft hands. When I remember to do that, I am far more likely to stay in control when conditions around me start to change. When you are on the lookout for moments of possibility, keeping soft eyes can help boost your powers of observation.

Using an Image or Talisman to Keep Your Focus

In the last chapter, I mentioned a consulting gig very early in my career, and I described how this group of some seventy men and women representing management and labor turned on me. I didn't know about paying attention to my breathing. I didn't know about soft eyes. I just stood there and took it, and it was not pretty.

To my credit, I did have the good sense to hire Lloyd Richards, the most experienced consultant I knew personally at the time. And he was a great guy. It came time for a break. Lloyd had been standing off to the side watching. I walked over to him. He smiled and asked, "How's it going?"

I said, "What do you mean how's it going? It's going to hell in a handbasket is how it's going! I'm being attacked out there. This meeting is ruined!"

He kept smiling and said, "No, it's not."

And then Lloyd gave me some of the best advice I have ever gotten in my life. He said, "Rick, this storm has been brewing for a very long time. And this event allowed those storm clouds to actually meet and collide. That created a lot of thunder and lightning. You didn't create that storm, but you are the highest point. Now you've got a choice. You can continue to stand there like an old oak tree and take all those hits of lightning, or you could imagine you're a lightning rod and allow all that electricity to go through you and into the ground."

I followed his advice and was able to imagine those bolts running through me into the ground. And that allowed me to stay relatively calm and use whatever skills I had to facilitate as effectively as I could.

That happened over forty years ago, and it is still vivid in my mind, and I continue to draw on that image in tough situations. You might consider asking yourself, what image or talisman can you call on to keep your focus where it needs to be?

Develop Your Observation Skills Easily

I have a suggestion, and it's one I hope you will take seriously. I encourage you to find situations where you can observe what's going on when you are not expected to respond. In other words, don't pick a time when you're actually leading something or expected to contribute to a conversation. Just give yourself the freedom to observe.

WATCH PEOPLE AS THEY INTERACT WITH EACH OTHER

Find places where you can observe easily. For example:

✔ Airports can be great places to watch people trying to influence each other. You'll have the opportunity to sit back and watch people getting stressed and engaging others in ways that are probably not going to be helpful to their cause.

✔ Go to a neighborhood park and watch pickup basketball, baseball, tennis, or pickleball. Try not to get wrapped up in the game. You're not there to watch the game itself. You're there to watch how people respond when a play goes badly or when one goes well.

✔ In a meeting where you are on the agenda to make a presentation later on, just sit back and observe before your time comes. Since nobody is expecting you to speak, you can just hang out and watch. Yogi would be happy.

✔ Say you're at a school play or recital where you're waiting patiently for your child—clearly the most talented of the bunch—to perform. In the meantime, look at all the stuff going on around the performance. The nervousness of the teacher who's directing this show. Or other parents or the kids on stage as they respond to what's going on around them.

In our culture, just observing may seem way too passive, but anyone who might be a fan of Ohno and his circle—or Yogi Berra—can see the value of just watching.

▶ I encourage you to print out a copy of the worksheet for Application Activity #2 so you can begin recording what you notice. You'll find it at www.rickmaurer.com/MofPResources.

Application Activity #3

IMAGINE WHERE OTHERS' ENERGY MIGHT BE AS YOU OBSERVE

In Chapter 1, I asked you to identify things you loved about a job you had. As you participate in a meeting, note the extent to which those items are present for you or not.

Then look around you and do your best to step into your colleagues' shoes and ask yourself if those positive things seem to be present in those people. You are only guessing where their energy might be, but that's plenty good enough for now.

▸ Remember, you can download all of the Application Activity worksheets at www.rickmaurer.com/MofPResources.

I hope you will keep the spirit of focused observation alive, not just as you read this book, but while you work with others as you plan and implement new changes and projects.

And then . . .
In the next chapter, I will invite you to begin to observe situations where you are actively involved. The purpose of this is to increase your ability to observe what's going on in the background and at the edges while you are counting how often players pass a ball. You will probably find it much more difficult to observe when you are actively engaged in the work. That's why the practice activities in this chapter are so important.

Key Points in Application Activity #2:
Watch People as They Interact with Each Other

→ During this activity, simply observe people in action. Try to avoid using some theory or psychological framework as you observe—just notice!

Key Points in Application Activity #3:
Imagine Where Others' Energy Might Be as You Observe

→ Step in your colleagues' shoes and ask yourself if the positive things you identified in Application Activity #1 are present. For now, simply observe.

CHAPTER 3

Sharpening Your Focus

"History repeats itself. So you might wanna pay attention."
–QUAVO, rapper, singer, songwriter

Just as a photographer might carry a kit bag filled with different types of lenses—telephoto, wide angle, and so forth—I find it helpful to have different lenses when I am observing and working with individuals and groups. A new lens often helps me see a situation more clearly from a different perspective and spot moments of possibility that I might otherwise miss.

Here are four of the lenses I like to use. I do not use all of them all the time, so you might pick one. Try it out. If something seems to be missing, adapt it or try something else.

✔ A variation on the Ohno Circle

✔ My own Three Levels of Support and Resistance

✔ Learning from what Zappos developed regarding motivation

✔ Stepping into others' shoes and doing the 180-degree switch

You may have lenses—points of view, theories, models—that you find useful. That's great. I hope you will continue using them. But please consider my warning later in the chapter about the possible limits of our favorite lenses.

The Ohno Circle

As you probably gathered in the previous chapter, I am a fan of the Ohno Circle. It speaks to the profound simplicity of Yogi Berra's comment, "You can observe a lot just by watching."

I find it refreshing in that, at its simplest, it involves watching with curiosity and interest. If you are working on a production line like Taiichi Ohno was, then your observations are likely to be filtered through LEAN or Six Sigma perspectives. (In plain language, LEAN means to cut out waste, keep ourselves lean, and Six Sigma means to measure quality out to six standard deviations. That is an amazingly high standard of quality.)

For the purposes of *Seizing Moments of Possibility*, I need lenses that can help me see where forward energy or support is continually building (or at least staying strong).

The Three Levels of Support and Resistance

I introduced this simple model in my 1996 book, *Beyond the Wall of Resistance*. It has changed some over the years, but I still think it is a useful way to look at situations where individuals and groups need to make decisions and carry them out together.

When people ask what I do for a living, I say that I focus on two questions:

Why do people support us?
Why do they resist us?

Exploring those questions has kept me busy for a lot of years.

The better we can see what causes resistance, the easier it is to build support for our ideas. In other words, if we understand the types of resistance, we also understand the other sides of those same coins—which is support for change.

A couple of fundamental things that we sometimes miss:

✔ Support and resistance are on a continuum, with strong support on one end and strong resistance on the other. I call this The Energy Bar™.

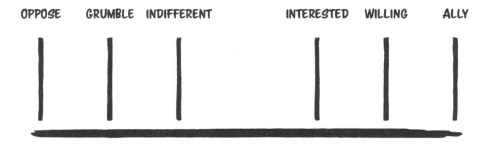

THE ENERGY BAR™

OPPOSE   GRUMBLE   INDIFFERENT   INTERESTED   WILLING   ALLY

Energy is always present, working either for us or against us. I saw a change management model that included a step labeled something like "Deal with Resistance." Resistance doesn't just appear at a set time (and neither does support). Energy is a dynamic force.

If you'd like to know more about The Energy Bar, please visit www.energybartools.com. You will find a simple tool to help you identify any gap in the energy you need and the energy you are likely to get. There are a lot of free resources on this site.

✔️ In my view, we have the best chance of building strong support by treating resistance (and those who resist) with interest and respect. At the beginning of this book, I asked you five questions. Number 2 read, "How willing are you to be influenced by the people you want to influence?" If you scored a 4 or 5 on that scale, then we are in agreement. If you scored 1 or 2, you are not likely to find the rest of this book useful. If you scored 3, stick around; maybe you'll like what you see.

Here are the three interlocking levels of support and resistance.

LEVEL 1: I Don't Get It.

Level 1 involves information: facts, figures, ideas. It is the world of thinking and rational action. It is the world of presentations, diagrams, and logical arguments.

Level 1 resistance may come from . . .

- Lack of information

- Disagreement with data

- Lack of exposure to critical information

- Confusion over what it means

Many make the mistake of treating all resistance as if it were Level 1.

Well-meaning leaders give people more information—hold more meetings and make more slide presentations—when, in fact, something completely different might be called for. In fact, if you keep pushing more facts and figures and slides onto people who already understand what you are talking about, you are likely to create resistance at Level 2 and maybe even Level 3.

Obviously, people do need to understand us. That's the positive side of Level 1. But what does "getting it" look like? People will ask intelligent questions based on what they understand. They connect the dots and begin to see the importance of what they are hearing. They can infer the implications of what all this information could mean.

LEVEL 2: I Don't Like It.

Level 2 resistance is an emotional reaction to a change. Blood pressure rises, adrenaline flows, and our pulse rate increases. It is based on fear: People are afraid that this change will cause them to lose face, status, control—maybe even their jobs.

Level 2 is not soft stuff. You can't say, "Just get over it" and expect people to reply, "Wow, thanks, I needed that." Level 2 runs deep. When it kicks in, we can feel like our very survival is at stake.

When Level 2 resistance is active, it makes communicating very difficult. When adrenaline shoots through our system, we move into fight-or-flight mode (or we freeze, like a deer in the headlights). And we stop listening. So no matter how terrific your presentation is, once people hear "downsizing," their minds (and bodies) go elsewhere. And that is uncontrollable. They are not choosing to ignore you, it's just that they've got more important things on their minds—like their own survival.

Organizations usually don't encourage people to respond emotionally, so employees tend to limit their questions and comments to Level 1 issues. They ask polite questions about budgets and timelines. So, it may appear that they are with you, but they're not. Maybe they are asking Level 1 questions hoping that you'll read between the lines and speak to their fears. And here is a really tricky part—they may not even be aware that they are operating on such a basic survival level.

The positive side of this emotional reaction is excitement, engagement, and hope. Remember, Level 2 is always alive, and if you can get its emotional energy working for you, you are on the way to building support for your project.

LEVEL 3: I Don't Like You.

In Level 3 resistance, people are not resisting the idea—in fact, they may love what you are suggesting. *They are resisting you.* Maybe their history with you makes them wary. Perhaps they are afraid that this will be "a flavor of the month" like so many other changes or that you won't have the courage to make the hard decisions to see this through.

But maybe it's not you. People may be resisting those you represent. The statement, "Hi, I'm from headquarters, and I'm here to help" often leaves people skeptical. If you happen to be that person from headquarters or IT or HR, you're going to have a hard time getting people to listen to you.

Lack of attention to Level 3 is a major reason why resistance flourishes and many changes fail. And it is seldom talked about. Many books on change talk about strategies and plans (all good stuff, to be sure) but most of this advice fails to recognize that lack of trust and confidence is a major reason why many changes fizzle out—or why we never get those people interested in what we have to say in the first place.

On the other hand, if the Level 3 reaction to you is positive, people may even give you the benefit of the doubt on an idea they find questionable. They go along because they trust you.

Whatever the reasons for deeply entrenched resistance, you can't afford to ignore it. As I said earlier, energy is always alive, working for or against you. The good news is that support comes from the other sides of the Levels 1, 2, and 3 coins. In other words, people get it, like it, and have trust and confidence in us.

Zappos' Model of Success

It can sometimes be difficult to pick out individual motivations when you are observing—or at least it is hard for me. Nevertheless, keeping in mind four themes that Zappos CEO Tony Hsieh (1973–2020) identified can be worthwhile.

Hsieh built Zappos up from a fairly simple online shoe store to an industry leader in clothing and accessories. He believed that happiness was key to the company's success. If employees were happy, they would do things to make customers happy. Those customers would not only come back again and again, but they would tell their friends.

He was not a fan of the psychology or the philosophy of happiness, but he was attracted to empirical research on what made people happy. He boiled what he learned down into four major categories:

1. Perceived Control. People have some control over the work they do.

2. Perceived Progress. People feel that they are making progress.

3. Connectedness. People are motivated by deep connections with others.

4. Being Part of Something Bigger Than Yourself. The longest-lasting type of happiness is about being part of something that has meaning for you [Hsieh, T. (2013) *Delivering Happiness: A Path to Profits, Passion and Purpose*. New York: Hachette, p 237.]

When they are working well, those four things can sound simple. When they are not, happiness and thus success are difficult to achieve.

I believe those four things can be a very helpful lens for spotting moments of possibility. I recall a series of planning meetings I attended some years ago. What makes me happiest about those meetings is that I never have to attend them again. Let's look at those regular meetings through the four items on Tony Hsieh's list.

1. I felt like I had some control, but there were forces on the floors above us that had much more control over what we were planning.

2. Progress was very slow. It seemed like we covered the same ground over and over again, and seldom in ways that actually improved the quality of what we were doing.

3. Connections with others happened in a way that worked for me personally but not for the work we were doing. Often the people with whom I felt a kinship became my allies in cynicism. They were the people I could turn to with a sarcastic comment or listen intently when they had something equally withering to say.

4. It seldom felt like the work we were doing—even when we were doing it well—amounted to much. I believed that what we "accomplished" could easily be changed or overridden by those higher up the food chain.

Just reading through my reactions to the Zappos list, I can see many lost moments of possibility while I was working in that group.

In Chapter 1, I asked you to think about a job that you loved. I chose a combo I performed with while I was in college as an example. I encourage you to go back to Application Activity #1 in Chapter 1 and see if most of Tony Hsieh's four items are present on your own list. My guess is that they are.

Step into Their Shoes

Years ago, I was making a presentation to an organization, speaking about support and resistance. During the presentation, someone raised his hand and said, "Rick, next week a bomb is going to drop." That got my attention. Others agreed with him, and someone asked, "What should we do?" I didn't know. I was simply there at the invitation of their consultant to make a presentation.

But since they were looking at me with puppy-dog eyes pleading for some magic answer, I had to do something. So I asked, "Does everyone here know somebody who will be coming to this meeting next week—where you'll be presenting your plan for this massive change?" Everybody said yes.

So I asked, "What's going to be on their minds when they come into the meeting room next Monday?" People started shouting out their responses faster than I could write, but as I was scribbling their answers on a flip chart, I realized how I might help.

I said, "Let's put these into categories. Which of the items on your list are Level 1 and have to do with information or lack of it? What items are Level 2 and are based on fear or excitement? And which of these are Level 3 and have to do with trust and confidence—or the lack of it?"

I chose a different color for each level, so that it would be easy to make sense of these results.

Once we color-coded the list by levels, someone immediately said, "Oh, that's why the bomb is going to drop!" He said that they had designed this meeting to deal with Level 1 issues—goals, objectives, timelines, and so forth. And yet, the list on the flipchart had very few Level 1 issues on it. The biggest issue was that people were afraid, and they didn't trust this planning team.

This simple activity allowed the planners to step into the shoes of the people they wanted to influence. And they did it easily. What they did next, though, had a huge impact on me and how I work.

They asked if they could take the next hour and redesign that meeting. Of course, we said yes, and for the next hour they did not call on us. They used what they had learned by stepping into the shoes of these stakeholders to redesign the meeting. (And, by the way, that meeting with stakeholders went very well.)

That experience is what prompted me to begin thinking about the importance of inviting groups like these to create lists. (For more on ways to create these lists, visit the Resources section.)

The 180° Switch

The 180° Switch is another easy way to figure out if people can step into the shoes of a person or a group that will be important during a big project or change. It's a simple thing you can do privately if you like. Or, you could do it with a partner.

Here's an example: A workshop participant said that he had a non-work-related situation. He was an avid baseball fan. He loved the Seattle Mariners team. They had just traded away Randy Johnson, a star pitcher.

I asked him to start telling me why the trade was a bad idea. At some point, at my choosing, I would say, "Switch." He had to switch his position by 180° and tell us why the trade was such a good idea. And then I would say, "Switch" and he would have to go back to telling us why it was a bad idea. This was a hard activity for him. You could almost see steam coming out his ears when he had to switch.

Having to switch positions quickly can be a powerful way to improve our ability to see situations from new perspectives. And you can test your knowledge of what's important to the people you want to influence by trying a 180° switch by yourself.

But what if you can't make a switch? Let's say that you simply can't see this issue through the eyes of the people who you want to influence. Unless you find a way to begin to see the world through their eyes, you will limit your ability to influence them.

Your Tried and True Lenses

You probably have a preferred way of looking at work situations. It may be using one of the lenses I talk about in this book, or you might like to look at the world through the lens of some personality, communication, or team development theory. Maybe you like to look at situations through lenses of diversity, equity, and/or inclusion. Any of these might work. But test your favorite lens and see if it helps you pick up any moments of possibility.

A Warning About Observing

Models and lenses are good things. They can help us perceive things that we might have missed and see situations with greater clarity, but they can also limit what we see. Too strong an attachment to one lens can get in the way of seeing gorillas in our midst. I recall someone asking me what my personality type was. I told her I'm a ZQKSJ. (I am making this classification up.) This person said, "You can't be an ZQKSJ." I said, "Yes I can. That description fits me." And she said, "No, you're wrong." While it is certainly possible that I was wrong, the bigger problem was that this person couldn't seem to think outside the constructs and constraints of her favorite theory. It was like she was trying to make everything—including me—fit within that tidy framework.

I encourage you to be willing to back off from your pet lens when evidence seems to question its value in understanding what's going on.

In the next chapter, I will show you some fairly easy ways of beginning to respond effectively to moments of possibility.

Application Activity #4

TRY OUT NEW LENSES WHILE OBSERVING

Select one of the ways of observing that sounds interesting but is relatively new to you. Let's say you pick the three levels of support and resistance. Find a situation to observe (it could even be a television drama). Observe that show or situation using the three levels as lenses. What do you see that indicates understanding—or lack of it? (That would be Level 1.) What do you see that indicates strong emotions either for or against the idea (Level 2)? What do you see that might indicate trust or lack of it (Level 3)?

What was easy about observing through that lens?

What was difficult?

Do you think it will be worth your while to use that model again as a new observational lens? Why or why not?

The purpose here is to find or refine a few lenses that can work for you.

▶ Remember, you can download all the Application Activity worksheets at www.rickmaurer.com/MofPResources.

I know that I have focused a lot on observing, but it is worth all that attention. Even though I believe everything I've written in these chapters, I still need to remind myself that I need to be able to observe or listen deeply. When I reflect on times when something didn't go well in a meeting or some other exchange with a person or group, it was often my failure to even notice juicy moments of possibility.

Key Points in Application Activity #4:
Try Out New Lenses While Observing

→ Select one of the ways of observing. For example: the Ohno Circle, Zappos' model of success, and so forth.

→ What was easy about observing through this lens?

→ What was difficult?

→ Do you think it will be worthwhile to use this model again as a new way to observe? Why or why not?

CHAPTER 4

Tweaking and Blending Energy into Existing Activities

"Vulnerability is the birthplace of innovation, creativity, and change."

BRENE BROWN, *The Power of Vulnerability*

If you tried out the observation activities I suggested in the previous chapters, you will likely have identified many moments of possibility. This chapter is where you can begin to put those sharp observations to work.

Think of "tweaking energy" as a way of making minor changes to existing activities. These small tweaks are relatively easy ways to take advantage of moments of possibility. Small changes can have a huge impact on increasing support and forward momentum.

Making small changes can allow you and another person or group to stay within your respective comfort zones—and that is critically important. (More about that later.) You are less likely to get pushback when you suggest a small way—a tweak—to increase participation or get feedback on some portion of the work.

Small changes can add up and begin to weaken that invisible wall that often separates participants and presenters. So, whether it is a large meeting, a conference call, coffee with your boss, or any other planned activity where you might be able to increase interest and support for your project or big change, tweaking could be a good place to begin.

Blending at Its Best

Blending energy into existing activities is a great way to begin to increase your capacity (and the capacity of others) to build a strong foundation for open communication and increased ownership in the quality of the work you are doing.

And blending with simple tweaks is also a safe way to see what works for you and for the people you are trying to influence.

I once attended an offsite event held by a client. Friday ended with a big dinner and social activities that lasted well into the night, so early Saturday was not an ideal time for anyone to make a presentation. But someone had to take that slot.

One of their colleagues had come up with a way to improve something in their organization. He was prepared. He had put together a logical and clear slide show. Since I had no role in that part of the program, I sat in back, fortified myself with coffee, and watched.

He began. His attention seemed to be entirely focused on the slides on his laptop screen. The audience could see the slides projected behind him. After a few minutes, I started looking around the room. A guy a couple rows in front of me was doing the crossword puzzle in the morning paper.

Others seemed to be checking their phones. Some walked to the back of the room where the coffee and pastries were set up. That made sense since it was early in the morning, but they stayed there and started talking (whispering, actually) to each other. The speaker seemed oblivious to what was going on. I don't think he noticed that he was losing the room.

Forty-five minutes later, he got to the final slide. He looked up and asked if there were any questions. No response. Nothing. He waited a few moments. He said thank you, closed his laptop, and left the stage. I doubt he knew why his presentation fell flat.

What if he had put in a note to himself to look up every few minutes and ask what people thought from time to time? Or added a slide or two with provocative questions and asked for reactions? What if he had learned his presentation so well that he didn't need to look at each slide so intently? What if he had asked the group to rate their enthusiasm for his idea? "Could I see a show of hands. . .?"

You can probably think of other moments of possibility that he might have considered. I am not suggesting that you try all these tweaks at once. Keep it simple and safe for everyone. Relative comfort is key to making this work.

Avoid Death by Slides by Thinking Ahead

Thinking ahead may be the easiest way to start tweaking.

Another client worked in an organization that almost demanded that everyone use PowerPoint. He told me it was a sign that you had spent time preparing your presentation. He knew this was kind of ridiculous, but he figured out how to play the game. He also knew that too many slides would wear people out, and his audience would get distracted, so instead of the typical fifty slides, he used five. Not only did he cover all the material, but he got a lot more interaction with the audience because there was room for it. This was a simple but effective tweak.

We need to keep our eyes open for moments of possibility. In this example, the presenter was able to think about ways to build in moments of possibility as he put together his presentation. Thinking ahead gives you time to consider some simple options. You can try them out in your head and even practice before the event. The actor Stanley Tucci said, "As an actor, the more prepared you are beforehand, the more spontaneous you can be." Like good actors, that planning allows us to be available for potential moments. Otherwise, we hide behind our scripts or slides.

The guy in the early Saturday morning time slot might have benefitted from even a few more minutes of prep time to consider his audience and the impact of doing his talk at eight a.m. knowing that some would be tired or even hung over.

Your Very First Tweak

You may have been capitalizing on these moments of possibility all along, but if this idea is new to you, here is a practical way to get started. In fact, you might be able to try it out today.

Choose a meeting or conference call in which you are in charge of at least a portion of the agenda.

Ask yourself, what would energize me? And then, what do I believe might energize others in this meeting?

What is one easy thing I could suggest or simply try out to see if it might add a spark of energy?

I encourage you to draw on what you know about yourself and your comfort level in meetings like this, and what you know about this group. These are some places that offer good potential for tweaks. I DO NOT offer them as one-size-fits-all suggestions, but merely as examples.

Places where I've seen small changes make a big difference:

- ✔ Big meetings
- ✔ Staff meetings
- ✔ Informal meetings
- ✔ Over coffee
- ✔ A portion of a regularly scheduled staff meeting
- ✔ Newsletters, e-mails, and texts
- ✔ And the list goes on

Yes, there is a place for special events that bring lots of people together to plan or critique ideas and plans. But don't start there. I have seen too many events where the leaders and their consultants (including me) get out over their skis. In other words, that hairy double black diamond slope looked so inviting, but we really should have started on the bunny slope.

Application Activity #5

LOOK FOR PLACES TO TWEAK AND BLEND

Identify where you want to start blending support or energy into activities.

Here are some tweaks you might consider, but please don't be limited by this list. And please don't try to cram too many new things into the meeting.

✔ Change the length of the meeting.

✔ Make sure everyone knows the purpose of the meeting and what you expect to achieve.

✔ Invite "the right people." That could include people who have the authority to make decisions. People who will have strong, valuable, and maybe even unsettling things to say. People who will have to work on this project. People who will have to implement all these ideas and make the effort a success.

✔ Serve refreshments after the meeting—and then be available to talk. No phones, text, or other distractions. Your job is to be available to listen and talk with people.

✔ Take breaks. Breaks are not a waste of time.

✔ Limit the number of slides.

✔ Find ways to engage people in meaningful ways. And those people get to determine what "meaningful" means to them.

✔ End the meeting by stating explicitly what the next steps will be. Leave ample opportunities for people to make comments and ask questions. (Avoid limiting their engagement to simply asking questions. This reinforces a power imbalance that will not help you build strong support.)

✔ And the list goes on. . .

▶ You'll find a worksheet at www.rickmaurer.com/MofPResources.

The Application Activity worksheet simply helps you keep the focus narrow and manageable.

Put Yourself in This Picture

Your own energy counts as well. The jargon in my field refers to it as "using yourself as an instrument." I know that sounds a bit pretentious, but it is worth paying attention to.

When I am in a meeting—no matter what my role is—I try to pay attention to my own energy. If I am getting bored, maybe others are as well. If I am getting engaged, maybe others are too. If I am confused, maybe others don't get it either. Notice that I use the word *maybe* in all those sentences. My awareness of my own reaction can be a very good barometer for imagining how others might be reacting, but I need to test those assumptions to make sure.

What to Avoid as You Start Finding Opportunities to Tweak and Blend

I got a call from a couple of guys I knew who are in an engineering department. They had an idea they wanted to present to an important group. They were concerned about the reaction they might get. They were afraid the audience might have strong Level 2 (emotional) and Level 3 (lack of trust) reactions.

They wanted suggestions on ways to get reactions in a way that would be productive. The 90-minute meeting was going to be held in a classroom with tiered, immovable seats, much like some university lecture halls.

I suggested that after they welcome people, they spend five to ten minutes presenting a high-level view of their idea.

Then I suggested that they ask people to turn to one other person and talk about their reactions to what they'd just heard. And then ask for reactions from the full group. These guys were silent for a few moments, and then they told me they couldn't do that.

I wondered why. This seemed like a simple, no-risk idea. It was the type of activity I frequently used in meetings. These guys told me that asking people to talk to each other would be "too touchy-feely." They couldn't take that chance.

Here is what I learned from that exchange. My comfort with that idea did not guarantee that my approach would be a good fit for them. I needed to be aware of textbook solutions or ideas that I thought were *brilliant* but might cause my clients to get all apoplectic. A tweak should be something small and reasonably comfortable for everyone involved. It was important that those two guys and I came up with something that would work for them and their audience.

Here's a short list of things to avoid when you want to tweak:

✔ Suggesting something small that you know is far outside the comfort zone of the other individual or group.

✔ Adding more work for people, such as adding time to the agenda or squeezing in just a few more key points during the meeting. Adding something is seldom a tweak—in fact, it can be more like a big pain. Tweaks should be tiny.

✔ Inflicting some one-size-fits-all technique on the group, simply because one size *doesn't* fit all.

Confusing Talking with Connecting

Please don't confuse merely talking about something as a tweak that can build support. One-way communication can be good for making points, but it can fall short when it comes to actually getting people interested and energized in what we have to say.

I recall a consulting assignment where we, the consulting team, offended our client. We realized our mistake, and one member of the consulting team agreed to make an apology and then facilitate a conversation with the client group. That seemed like a good idea.

But he never shut up. Someone would ask a question or make a statement. He would get defensive and talk and talk at them. He would explain to them why they were wrong!

That approach didn't go over. If he, or any one of our team, had apologized sincerely and then listened to the group openly, I believe the tension would have subsided pretty quickly. As it turned out, our mistake infected all our subsequent conversations with the client.

Application Activity #6

EVALUATE HOW IT WENT

I hope your experience is different from mine, but I rarely see people debrief meetings of any length or size in ways that give them valuable information. I do hear: "Good slides" or "Nice presentation." Nothing wrong with those comments, but they don't focus on what should be important.

What is important? *Did this meeting blend in support so that you could see (or feel) energy building in a way that moved things forward even a little bit?*

Pretty simple, right? And that's the point. You want to evaluate how you did quickly while the meeting is still fresh in your mind.

After trying out a tweak, ask yourself:

- What was your intention when you made that small change?

- How did it go? If it worked well, identify why it worked so well. If it fell flat, identify why it never took hold. And if it really bombed, what was going on?

- How do you know? If you are a person who tends to see the bright side of everything, congratulations. Now get real. What's your data to tell you that it worked? And if you usually see "what's wrong with this picture?" then get real. What's the data to support your conclusions? The goal is to try things out so you can learn.

- And the big question is, What did you learn that might be useful next time?

It's Time to Make Tweaking a Part of Your Repertoire

You could read more books, attend more training, watch YouTube videos, and all those things might be helpful. But I believe that perhaps the best thing you can do is to practice in real time with real people. My friends in the gestalt community often refer to this as *safe emergencies*. Because you are doing something small—a tweak—you can keep the risk low for yourself and the people you want to influence. These are not role plays (which can come across as bad, phony acting) but real exchanges with other people. That's where the potential excitement and anxiety (or emergency) comes in.

Application Activity #6 can be helpful as you look for places to blend in small changes to other existing activities. Please feel free to make multiple copies of this application worksheet.

A Small Change Can Have a Big Impact

You may not need one more example of the impact of small changes, but I love the following story and thought you might as well. And it is a good way to end this chapter.

A C-level executive in a major corporation often kicked off training sessions for up-and-coming managers. He didn't send an assistant or ask them to play a prerecorded welcome message. He told audiences that he wanted to be there because "You are the future of our organization." Then he gave them a choice.

He said he would be glad to show the PowerPoint presentation their company had prepared for Wall Street. He said it provided a good picture of the business landscape, the opportunities and threats that might be on the horizon, and so forth. "Or," he said, "I could turn off the computer and simply address your questions for the next hour." I was in the back of the room at least a dozen times when he gave groups that choice. I never saw a group vote to see the slide show. Never. And you might have guessed that his credibility was very high in that organization.

Others told similar stories about this executive. People loved him and working for and with him.

In the next chapter, I will show you how to begin to identify places to blend in energy at every step—every meeting or call—from the beginning to the end of your big new initiative.

Key Points in Application Activity #5:
Look for Places to Tweak and Blend

→ Identify where you want to start blending support or energy into activities.

→ Identify one thing that you want to try. (See the list of possible things you could tweak.)

→ What's the context? (a presentation, a staff meeting, monthly reports, etc.)

→ What do you want to try to improve by blending energy in a small way?

→ What will this tweak look like?

Key Points in Application Activity #6:
Evaluate How It Went

After trying out the tweak, ask yourself:

→ What was your intention when you made the small change?

→ How did it do? Why did it work or not?

→ How do you know if it went well or not?

→ What was your own energy like when you introduced this tweak?

→ What did you learn that might be useful next time?.

CHAPTER 5

Putting Fresh Batteries into Your Plans

"We should learn from the mistakes of others.
We don't have time to make them all ourselves."

–GROUCHO MARX

Seizing moments of possibility—no matter how small—is the heart of building support for our ideas, big projects, and organizational changes.

There are often hundreds of these moments of possibility during the life of a big project. Many of the moments are small and easy to miss, some are big, but all can help create and sustain energy if we know how to tap into them.

This chapter is all about taking the necessary steps to blend the power of these moments of possibility into your existing plans. The focus is on looking for ways to spark energy and momentum into all those activities that fill up our calendars.

Think about a recent project that didn't go so well and consider the wasted opportunities: people attending meetings that lacked a clear purpose, leaving key individuals and groups out of the loop, allowing bureaucracy to fiddle with plans and sap any excitement or energy from them, and the list goes on and on.

In this chapter, I will show you:

✔ How to determine if your existing plan is likely to help you build and sustain forward momentum from beginning to end

✔ How to anticipate and avoid the common errors that can drain energy

✔ How to add vitality to your existing plan

✔ How to know if you are actually getting the energy you need at every step along the way

✔ How to determine if your existing plan is likely to help you build and sustain forward momentum from beginning to end

It is likely that you will need energy working for you from the beginning through to the successful completion of your new idea, project, or big change.

I have identified four major pockets or centers of potential energy in the life of a major change or big project. Remember, energy is always alive, and it is working either for or against you.

POCKET OF ENERGY 1: People See and Feel a Sense of Urgency That Something New Is Needed

The people who will need to support your project must feel a sense of urgency—a desire to do something to meet this challenge or take advantage of this opportunity. Just telling people that something new is needed is seldom sufficient. Data doesn't put fire in our bellies.

Here is a place where I like to apply the three levels of support and resistance that I covered in Chapter 3. Level 1: People understand what you are talking about. That's good, but. . . Level 2 is where the fire in the belly comes in. People feel the need to change in their bones. And they trust the people telling them all this. That's Level 3.

Sadly, leaders often skip over this critical portion of the work and move right into planning. In fact, some plans don't even cover what to do to help people see and feel that something new is needed.

When this occurs, organizations miss the potential burst of energy that can come when they successfully *create a sense of importance and urgency.*

POCKET OF ENERGY 2: Find Ways to Get People Engaged in the Changes That Affect Them

This is what you might be calling the planning stage. It is the time when you decide how you will address a threat or opportunity. You set goals and objectives, develop a master plan, and begin to create tactical plans, which should lead seamlessly into the next phase in your work.

Your written plan probably includes a lot of steps. You need to decide if these are the right steps for the type of project you are considering. But your plan also needs to include ways to capitalize on the moments of possibility in this potentially powerful pocket of energy. For example, let's say that we want to create a financial management plan that gives leaders and financial services professionals easy and rapid access to critical information when they need it. A vendor shows us a plan that promises to provide "easy and rapid access to critical information." We should look at the details of that plan to see if it is likely to cover everything needed in order to effectively plan, implement, and embed this new system into how people access financial data. And, in addition, we need to look at that same plan and ask ourselves if those steps are likely to build and sustain energy and forward momentum from beginning to end.

POCKET OF ENERGY 3: Handle Implementation and Rollout so People Know Their Contributions Are Valuable

In many organizations, this stage is taken for granted. Leaders move on to what seem like more pressing concerns and assign implementation to others without giving them the ongoing support and resources they will need to make plans to come to life.

I was working with project leaders in a large organization. I asked them which stages of change projects they liked to work on. All of them said making a case for the project (that's Pocket of Energy #1) and planning it (that's Pocket #2.) No one chose the third pocket. I asked, "What do you do when a project gets to implementation?" One guy said, "We hand it off." Others nodded in agreement. So I asked, "And who do you hand it off to? I don't see anyone standing there." Silence, then someone said, "That's our problem. We just assume others will pick up the ball—but they don't."

Successful implementation requires more than a smooth handoff. You also need to be sure that those people know that they are critical to a successful outcome—and that the project is still a top priority for the organization.

POCKET OF ENERGY 4: Ensure That the Change (or Project) Results in Significant Value—and Everyone Involved Can See How Important All Their Work Has Been

It seems odd to me, but some organizations do a fine job getting through the first three pockets of energy, but they ignore this final one. They may set lofty goals, but the plan offers no help in turning implementation (Pocket 3) into something of real value.

I was talking with one leader who said they often did a good job of measuring implementation. Did the projects come in on time? Within budget? Did they install the software and get the bugs out? Did people get the training they needed? But that's where things stopped. They measured success by how well they completed all the detailed work of implementation (Pocket 3). But they never looked at the larger picture they were trying to accomplish.

When personal computers started appearing on people's desks, many ignored them or used them as little as possible. I believe it was Ken Blanchard who said that these new desktop computers were "the world's most expensive paperweights." Let me put his astute observation into my own language. Organizations saw the potential value in using computer power (Pocket 1), so they purchased computers for their people (Pocket 2). They trained the staff how to use them (Pocket 3). And then they hoped for the best.

Hope is not a plan. Make sure you don't just hope for the best.

How to Anticipate and Avoid the Common Errors That Can Drain Energy

Begin by thinking about a project that was similar to the one you are about to lead. Perhaps it was a new waste reduction process or quality improvement or reorganization.

You will probably be able to plot the flow of that energy on something I call the Batteries Not Included™ Map.

Here are three common examples of energy maps. The map you create may look similar to or quite different from any of these examples. But thinking about past changes that went well—or didn't—can help you anticipate and often avoid drops in energy.

1. A BIG BANG APPROACH TO CHANGE

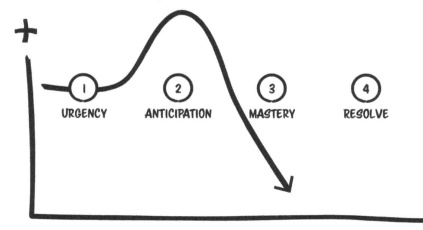

BATTERIES NOT INCLUDED MAP™

+

① URGENCY   ② ANTICIPATION   ③ MASTERY   ④ RESOLVE

In this map, you can see that a lot of effort went into a big planning event. Lots of people. Lots of active involvement. When a friend left a meeting like this, she said, "It's like I was walking on air. We did great work." And sometimes those big events can be catalysts for moving ahead with a lot of forward momentum.

But this example shows a different outcome. Energy peaked during the big event, and then nothing happened for weeks. By then, the energy had sunk to a dangerous low. When I explain the Big Bang Approach to clients, they often laugh and nod in recognition.

2. A PROJECT ON LIFE SUPPORT

You'll note that this dotted line never moves up very high. In fact, it is close to flatlining and dying. There is just enough energy to keep things moving forward in a halting fashion. In some instances, energy gradually drops, and the project dies a quiet death. Other times, the project actually makes it to Pocket 4, but the results are often weak and hardly worth the effort to get there.

A CEO once told me that all he was getting from his staff on a new project was "malicious compliance." That is a perfect way of describing this type of energy.

3. A SUCCESSFUL FLOW OF ENERGY

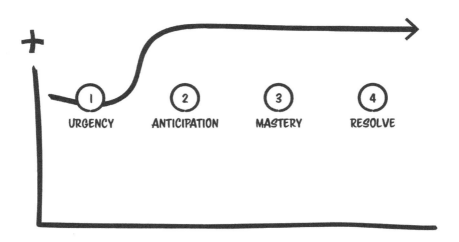

In this map, people saw and felt a need for something new right from the beginning (Pocket 1). Notice how the horizontal bar rises pretty quickly. They were ready to roll up their sleeves and plan this thing. Energy during Pocket 2 remained high. When they moved to Pocket 3, the handoff from planning to implementation went smoothly. Think of runners in a relay race handing off the baton without dropping it or losing a step. And then, they moved seamlessly from implementation into working to get significant value from what they had created (Pocket 4).

USING THE BATTERIES NOT INCLUDED MAP

You probably noticed that I drew only one line for each of those scenarios. There is a reason for that. I am just tracking the movement of the project itself and not the energy of any single stakeholder. When you are creating your own map, you might consider tracking the flow of support and forward momentum for a number of stakeholders to see how their respective energy ebbs and flows. If one group—let's say the planning group that you are part of—is excited and enthusiastic, that could give you a false sense of how the collective energy was moving. By mapping how the energy of other stakeholder groups is flowing, you can get a more complete, realistic picture.

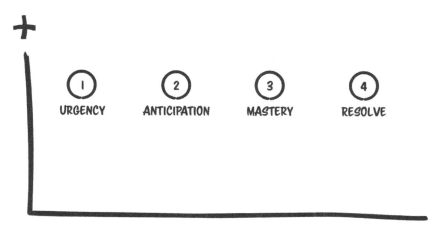

▶ You will find blank Batteries Not Included Maps as well as Application Activity #7 guidance for completing your own map at www.rickmaurer.com/MofPResources.

I encourage you to complete that map before you go on to the next section of this chapter.

How to Add Vitality to Your Existing Plan

Read through your current plan with the flow of energy in mind.

Just a reminder, my ideas will not help you determine the technical steps that need to be part of your plan. I will assume that you've decided on a plan that looks like it will take you where you want to go. If so, now it is time to make sure that energy is blended in, an integral part of the plan itself.

But what if you don't have a plan yet? Then I suggest the following steps to help you create a plan that already includes ways to engage people from beginning to end. I strongly suggest finding ways to blend energy in at every step rather than relying on a few big events.

Be careful. It is common to look at plans you are considering and see just the technical elements. For instance, does the plan offer a detailed guide to building X, to reducing waste in Y, to increasing market share in Z? That is important data, but it's not enough. Don't allow the importance of the technical details to overshadow the equally important aspects of interest, excitement, and commitment.

Read through your plan at whatever pace works for you. Imagine that you are following a storyline. You probably don't need a lot of details during this read-through; skimming might work just fine.

WHAT IS MY/OUR OWN REACTION TO OUR EXISTING PLAN

Pay attention to your own interest and energy as you read through the plan. The Application Activity includes all the items below.

✔ Where did you lose interest or energy?

✔ Where did your interest or energy grow? (You got excited, intrigued, engaged.)

✔ Then ask yourself, why did my own energy go down? Why did it go up?

✔ Now look at your entire plan as you might look at a roadmap that covers a lot of territory. Then ask:

- If you follow the plan just as it's written, will you be successful and stay within the time deadlines and budget?

- Are there places where energy drops significantly? Why do you think it might drop? What can you do to avoid that shift in energy by *Seizing Moments of Possibility* along the way?

- Might it be possible that the energy might never rise to a level that will do you any good?

✔ Drawing on what you already know about building support, what you've observed (Chapters 2 and 3), and what you've tried out (Chapter 4), how can you blend support into the plan before any problems with indifference or resistance ever occur?

If you find that there is nothing in your current plan to help you harness a positive flow of energy, then you might need to add additional steps. But please be careful. Adding steps can be helpful, or they can eat up precious time and energy.

I like to create a map so I can see where energy in a plan is likely to rise and fall. Thinking through my own reactions can often help me avoid problems before they ever become problems.

How to Know if You Are Actually Getting the Energy You Need to Move Projects from A to Zed

In the final question for each of the pockets of energy, I asked you to identify how you will know you're getting the energy you need. Seriously consider creating an informal Energy GPS tool to track the movement of energy. Too often, I've worked on (or led) projects where we just assumed we were on track. Sometimes that worked out, but other times everyone was surprised. We've got to know where we are in as close to real time as possible.

When I hike in wilderness areas, I cannot access GPS, so I have to create my own homemade tracking system. I make sure that I get my hands on the best map I can find for an area that is called a wilderness. (Sometimes the maps are poor, but usually I can find someone who knows those hills and valleys. That person's stories become my GPS tool.) As much as possible, I want to be able to look at the map (or read the notes the local expert gave me) to tell if I am going in the right direction and if my pace is going to get me to a good place to camp before nightfall.

I don't want to wait until I'm three days into a hike and running low on food to find out that I made a huge wrong turn two days before.

Just like the GPS in my car, I want to know where I am in real time. Waiting for some big employee survey to come along six months from now means that I could have missed a lot of exits and made a lot of wrong turns.

However I go about tracking energy, I want to know where things are with regard to Level 1, 2, and 3 issues. Do people get it? Like it? Trust me? (You might want to review the portion of Chapter 3 which covers the three levels.)

Putting Your Energy Plan to Use

I hope you will consider the Application Activities in this chapter as living documents. In other words, as conditions change, so do the opportunities and the challenges.

Application Activity #9

CREATE AN ENERGY GPS TOOL

Creating an Energy GPS tool that works for you may be the most important thing you can do as you begin to blend support and forward momentum into your plans. It's one thing to congratulate ourselves for the great work we just did, but quite another to get feedback that people didn't have a clue what we were talking about. I've been there. It's painful, but necessary.

Please take a little time to begin to create an informal GPS tracking device. Application Activity #9 will give you some ideas on easy ways to begin to make sure you are on or off course.

▶ Look for more info on creating the GPS device at www.rickmaurer.com/MofPResources.

In the Final Thoughts section that closes this book, I focus on how to make attention to moments of possibility a part of who you are rather than something you need to remind yourself about.

Key Points in Application Activity #7:
Using the Batteries Not Included Map™

Please watch the short video where I explain how I use the Batteries Not Included Map. You will find the video at www.rickmaurer.com/MofPResources.

Key Points in Application Activity #8:
What Is My/Our Reaction to the Existing Plan?

→ Pay attention to your own interest and energy as you read through the plan. (See list of questions to ask yourself.)

→ Consider creating a map that tracks how you think energy might rise and fall when you use your plan.

→ Using the map you just created as a guide, identify places where you can add energy or forward momentum into how you enact the plan.

Key Points in Application Activity #9:
Create an Energy GPS Tool

→ Create an Energy GPS. I include a list of ways that others have created to track energy in real time. (See the long list in this section of the chapter.)

Some Final Thoughts on Finding Even More Moments of Possibility

"I've learned that people will forget what you said, people will forget what you did, but people will never forget how you made them feel."

–MAYA ANGELOU, American Poet

U p until this point, we've focused on paying attention to moments of possibility when we want to build support for some idea or big project at work. I believe taking what you've learned in the preceding chapters seriously can be very beneficial. But . . . there is a limitation if you stop right there.

Moments of possibility can surprise us, catch us off guard. That's when it becomes clear that we have failed to see or make use of potential energy that is right in front of us. This is true at work, at home, and on the highway.

The Beginnings of a Success Story

My friends will tell you that I have never been a patient driver. When someone cuts me off or does something I consider bone-headed, I draw on language I learned hanging out in barracks or dorm rooms as a young man. I have an amazingly rich but unprintable vocabulary.

One night, my wife and I were driving home, and someone cut me off. This time I even rolled the window down so that the driver wouldn't miss a moment of my stellar prose. Kathy reminded me that where we lived, people were allowed to carry loaded weapons in their vehicles. She went on to say that she didn't want to be in the car with me when I was that uncontrollable.

That got my attention.

I had been dabbling at mindfulness practice for a while, just paying attention to my breath when I woke up in the morning. Even though I wasn't doing this practice every day, I started to notice a slight difference in how I responded in stressful situations and when there were a lot of potential distractions. I decided to make these mindfulness sessions a regular part of my morning routine just to see if that might help.

I noticed that when I got into the car for a trip into the city or onto the Beltway around Washington, DC (a nasty stretch of highway designed to enrich people's vocabularies), I could feel my shoulders begin to rise and tense. And this often happened even before I got out of our driveway. Seriously!

But that attention to tension actually helped me stay a bit calmer. Sometimes, even out on the Beltway, I could feel my upper body tense. In those moments, I just allowed my muscles to relax. Often, that's all that was needed for me to continue the drive with some degree of calmness.

In other words, I had created a simple discipline of mindful breathing practice for myself. Nothing fancy, just paying attention as I breathed in and out.

Yes, things still do catch me off guard more often than I would like, but these rich-vocabulary moments don't occur nearly as often—and these days I am far more likely to catch myself before I go too ballistic.

Driving a car like a maniac in traffic isn't the same as working on a project team, but there are similarities. When our minds are filled with anything, it makes it difficult to take in new information, even if it is right in front of us.

When we walk into a meeting or pick up a phone, we may be focused on one thing—let's say getting through the agenda quickly or making sure that every region has time to give its quarterly report or hearing some critical financial news from the sales department. Of course, that is fine, but when we have such a laser-like focus, we risk missing things. We miss seeing moments of possibility.

Creating the Capacity to Recognize and Respond to Moments of Possibility

I encourage you to not limit your attention to moments of possibility to when you are working on a big project. Opportunities for boosting energy and attention are everywhere, like when the phone rings while you are working on something important, a chance meeting in a hallway as you are rushing somewhere, coming home from work and entering an environment that seems worlds away from the one that is still occupying your attention, or driving the Beltway.

I truly believe that being open to these moments makes life and relationships richer. I have found that this often helps me at work or driving or talking with someone on a plane.

Here are a few simple things you might consider trying out:

✔ Practice breathing mindfully. This is a deceptively simple activity, but in my experience, it can be a foundation for being open to those moments of possibility.

If you conduct a Google or YouTube search on "mindful breathing" or "mindfulness," you will find a rich trove of ways to use your breath to become more open to what's going on in the moment. And these suggestions are often free and easy to try out.

If paying attention to your breath is new to you, start small. If you can spare five minutes, great. If all you've got is two minutes, then take two minutes. Personally, I like to do a practice like this for about 20 minutes in the early morning. But if that seems way too long, then start with an amount of time that feels right.

Within a short time, you are likely to find that you approach meetings and other interactions with people more calmly. You may notice that you are more aware of the situation, noticing things that you might otherwise have missed.

And here is where I think it gets fascinating: You may grow less concerned with forcing your position on others. You may notice that you are still speaking clearly but with less of a hard-sell vibe.

✔ Pay attention to your body. I mentioned my questionable driving behavior. I started to notice that my shoulders rise up, my neck tightens, my jaw might start to clench just a tiny bit. I notice that I am holding the steering wheel more tightly.

And just by noticing all that, the tension often subsides.

✔ Take a quick break in the action.

The fabled comic Groucho Marx always had a cigar in his hand. Whether it was in an early movie or when he was on television, the cigar was there. He had a television game show called *You Bet Your Life*. The game was quite insignificant. The reason many watched was to hear Groucho banter with guests. He was very funny and could make devastatingly witty remarks. According to George Fenneman, his announcer on the show, Groucho often used the cigar to buy time.

If he couldn't think of a good line, he would lean back, take a puff, and slowly bring the cigar down. The audience would begin laughing while Groucho was still thinking what he was going to say next.

I am not suggesting you take up cigar smoking. Taking a sip of water can work just as well. That pause—any pause—gives you a few moments to relax.

✔ Use a physical reminder.

It is easy for me to get intimidated by the audience when I play jazz gigs. If I am not careful, I will play it safe. I will improvise easy-to-digest solos. Nothing offensive, but also nothing much to get interested in either.

I have a photo of Groucho's brother Harpo on my music stand. It is from the movie, *A Night at the Opera*. In the picture, Harpo is sitting in an orchestra pit holding a trombone backwards. The picture is silly and absurd, and it makes me smile every time I look at it. (In fact, I am smiling as I write this sentence. How about that?)

And that smile usually relaxes me.

✔ Have a role model in mind.

When I first started consulting on bigger projects and projects that tended to have a lot of emotional static going on in meetings, I thought about a fellow consultant whom I admire.

Often, I would silently say to myself, *What would that person do?* Nothing spooky happened. No rainbows or unicorns were harmed in this little activity. But I would often relax a bit, and I would almost instantly know what to do. Of course, I knew what to do all along, but the tension of the moment had blocked those thoughts from my little brain.

✔ Go back to the well.

This one doesn't work quite so well in the moment, but I have found it helpful as I get ready for important meetings or events. I go back to books, articles, and even sentences I've underlined that have influenced me. This gives me an opportunity to bask in the wisdom in those pages. And often, it is wisdom that I had underlined and then forgotten.

As I was preparing to write this short book, I went back to some books I had read long ago. I didn't expect to lift anything from those pages, but they did help me focus and remind myself why I was writing this book in the first place.

Thanks for reading my book. I hope you found it useful. If you have questions or comments, please don't hesitate to contact me. I would love to hear from you.

Rick Maurer

Resources

All nine of the Application Activities can be accessed at www.rickmaurer.com/MofPResources.

CHAPTER 1: Why Is Lack of Energy So Deadly—and How Can You Avoid the Problems It Creates?

- Application Activity #1: Quick Ways to Identify What Gets People Excited and Engaged

- Link to my white paper titled *Are All-Hands Meetings Worth the Bother? http://rickmaurer.com/wp-content/uploads/2018/10/All-Hands-Meetings-White-Paper.pdf*

CHAPTER 2: Spotting Moments of Possibility

- Taiichi Ohno. A Google search on the Toyota Production System will lead you to a lot about Ohno and the Ohno Circles.

- Daniel J. Simons, *The Monkey Business Illusion*. https://www.youtube.com/watch?v=IGQmdoK_ZfY Please honor Dr. Simons' copyright. He posted this video for personal use and not for broadcast or use in training sessions. Thanks.

- Reference to John Mariotti and Huffy comes from the article I wrote for the *Caught in the Middle Newsletter* 4/1993. Sadly, it is way out of print.

- Chris Argyris conducted important research on executive teams. He has plenty of papers, books, and YouTube interviews.

- Dr. Debbie Crews's research: *What Should Be Going on in Your Brain During Golf.* https://golfsciencelab.com/golf-state/

- David Kohn, "What Athletes See". *The Atlantic Monthly*, 11/18/2015. The article covers research on "the quiet eye" and includes quotes from Dr. Joan Vickers, the study's primary author. https://www.theatlantic.com/health/archive/2015/11/what-athletes-see/416388/

- Application Activity #2: Watch People as They Interact with Each Other

- Application Activity #3: Imagine Where Others' Energy Might Be as You Observe

CHAPTER 3: Sharpening Your Focus

- You can learn much more about The Energy Bar at www.energybartools.com.

- "Resistance to Change – Why It Matters and What to Do About It" is a short article I wrote about the three levels. www.rickmaurer.com/wrm

- You will find the e-book *The Magic List* at: http://rickmaurer.com/magic-list/.

- Application Activity #4: Try Out New Lenses While Observing

CHAPTER 4: Tweaking and Blending Energy into Existing Activities

- Application Activity #5: Look for Places to Tweak and Blend
- Application Activity #6 Evaluate How It Went

CHAPTER 5: Putting Fresh Batteries into Your Plans

- Application Activity #7: Using the Batteries Not Included™ Map
- This doc includes a blank copy of the Batteries Not Included Map as well as suggestions for using this tool. Please feel free to make copies for your personal use. You may use it for your own planning or your work with a planning or executive team. Do not make copies of the Batteries Not Included Map for presentations, coaching, or consulting without my permission. (When in doubt, send me a note and we can talk. Thanks.)
- Application Activity #8: What is My/Our Reaction to the Existing Plan?
- Application Activity #9: Create an Energy GPS Tool

Some Final Thoughts on Finding Even More Moments of Possibility

- The Resources link includes a short list of some of the ideas and tools that help me try to stay more present.

Keeping This Approach Alive

As you and others apply what's in this book, I am certain that I will be adapting what you've just read. Please let me know how you have applied these ideas. What's worked? What hasn't? And how have you adapted my ideas? I will do my best to pass along what I learn from you. Thanks.

Rick Maurer
rick@rickmaurer.com

Thanks to Those Who Helped Me Create This Book

I started writing this book long before I ever knew I was going to write it. Four years ago, I started exploring the notion of unforced errors when we try to influence others. (Calling something an unforced error comes from sports. It is an avoidable mistake.) That grew into the Batteries Not Included Map™ which tracks the flow of energy up, down, and forward. Then I started combining those ideas with ways we could enhance forward momentum at every moment during the life of a big project or organizational change.

During all that time, I kept reaching out to people. I conducted interviews. Sent out questionnaires. Held free interactive webinars. Talked with people. Some intrepid clients even let me try out my ideas. Basically, I explored and asked a lot of questions of a lot of people. It was a great process. It is how I learn best.

I realized as I was putting this thank-you page together that I have gotten advice and support from people in well over twenty countries on four continents. I owe a lot to a lot of people. And I know that I am truly fortunate. Some made single comments that helped me clarify places where I was stuck. Others provided challenges and feedback. Others told me success stories and gave me examples of things that hadn't work. Thank you. (And my thanks to those people I inadvertently let off this list. I apologize. I am not great at keeping detailed notes. Just remind me so I can add your name to the list.) – Rick Maurer

Finn Bech Andersen

Henrik Horn Andersen

Mette Aagaard Andersen

Morten Kamp Andersen

Yannis Angelis

Chuck Appleby

Hans Arnbjerg

Dean Athanassiades

Melanie Audette

Jeff Bailey

Laura Barnard

Liz Barron

Kathy Bernhard

Parag Bhatnagar

Mette Bjerrum

Jim Blasingame

Lon Blumenthal

Lisbeth Borup

Jerry Bresee

Romy Brock

Brian Brooks

Dr. Douglas M. Brown

Linda Brown

Patti Brown

John Bryan

Heather Bryant

Michael Chirichello

Hui Wang Christiansen

Dr. Karen Cochran

Jean Coles

Kate Colson

Ian Cook

Chet Daigle

Kim Davenport, PhD

Joanne Daykin

Helena Demuynk

Robert Dickman

Marykate Dougherty

Rich Drinon

Hashem ElAssad

Ursula Erasmus

Barbara Feldman

Renë Jon Figgë

Justine Childs Friedman

Noemi Friexes

Michael Fullan

Sean Gaffney

Gary Gilligan

JoAnn Gorman

Przemyslaw Gowronski

Daniel Graham

Stan Grett

Vinay Gunther

Sofie Halkjaer

Mike Halus

Alan Harkness

Christian Harpelund

Kaaren Hilsen

Marianne Hinge

Neil Hodgson

Eric Honour

Khailaa Hosny

Louise Neel Høyer

Ken Hultman

Matthew Hunter

Jim Jenkins

Henrik Julin

Jarmo Jussinoja

Matt Kayhoe

Birgitte Kjaersgaard

Per Klingenberg

Gene Knott

Mark Lambert

Darryl A. Lansey

John Ledwith

Ron Leeman

Glenn Leppo

Dr. Laurie Lippin

Mary Lippitt

Roland Loup

Anna Katrine Lund
Dave Luke
Carolyn J. Lukensmeyer
Shannon Maginn
Kari Malinen
John Mariotti
Josef Martens
Patrick Masterson
Ric Matthews
David Maurer
Rhodri Meredith
Michael McFaul
J.R. McGee
David McLean
Jacquie McLemore
Mariam Mellouli
Tom Mierzwa
C.G. Mistry
Thomas Meylan
Michele Monetti
Cliff Moyce
Jose Morales
Steve Mousseau
Ronda Mullen
Jules Myers
Joanne Myles
David Newman
Caroline G. Nicholl
Sharon Nichols
Fred Nickols
Phil Nimtz
Dave Noll
Rebecca Osborne
Sharon Parker
Bill Palmer
Bev Patwell
Craig Petrun
Dave Papenmeier
Wendy Penry
LeRoy Pingho

Greta Rask
Frik Reynecke
Sharon Lebovitz Richmond
Borka Richter
Elizabeth Roll
Ross Roxburgh
Tine Rosenblum
Sami Saren
John Scherer
Larry Schmid
Rick Seikaly
Dr. Carolyn Slocombe
Darwin Smith
Liselotte Sondergaard
Leif Sorensen
Bertolt Stein
Jim Stockmal
Ian Sturgess
Emie Timmerman
Jolene Tornabeni
Barbara Trautlein
David Verble
Sille van Loon
Ron Vaughan
Kathy Vizachero
Gary Weisenborn
Paul White
W. David Williams
Dr. Abbe Winter
Nora Wolfson
Dave Wollert
Ye Xiao
Karen Zanetti
David Zinger
and Jim Zucco.

Special thanks to Leslie Stephen and Amanda Coffin for editing and Jamie Tipton for designing this book and its cover.

About Rick Maurer

Rick works with leaders who see big changes and projects as opportunities to engage people in the changes that will affect them. These leaders know that change can actually boost morale and commitment to the organization and the work.

He calls his approach Change without Migraines™! His opinion has been sought by *NBC Nightly News*, CNBC, BBC, *Fortune, The Wall Street Journal, USA Today, Industry Week, The Economist, Nation's Business, Fast Company, The Washington Post, Investor's Business Daily*, many trade and business publications and broadcast media.

His other books include *Beyond the Wall of Resistance, Why Don't You Want What I Want?, Feedback Toolkit, Building Capacity for Change Sourcebook*, and *Caught in the Middle*. He helped his friend Karl Berger write *The Music Mind Experience* which was published in 2020.

www.rickmaurer.com

ORDERING INFORMATION

The e-book version of *Seizing Moments of Possibility* is free and only available from my website.

If you would like multiple copies of the print version, please give me a call and I can tell you the price for paperback copies. Thanks.

MY WORK

Virtually all of my work focuses on the ideas and tools covered in this book.

In the beginning of the book, I asked you five questions:

- ✔ How important will it be for you to build support and strong forward momentum on big projects?
- ✔ How willing are you to be influenced by the people who you want to influence?
- ✔ How would you rate the importance your organization gives to building and sustaining strong support?
- ✔ To what extent do you believe that building support begins with you?
- ✔ How would you rate your effectiveness in this area?

Would you like you and your organization to improve in any of those areas? If so, give me a call. We might be a good fit for each other. I offer short presentations like keynote speeches, strategic work sessions to help executive and planning teams begin to apply the ideas in this book, and relevant group and individual coaching.

Rick Maurer
703 200-3074 (US)
www.rickmaurer.com

CPSIA information can be obtained
at www.ICGtesting.com
Printed in the USA
BVHW021945030322
630524BV00004B/67